THE POWERFUL ARMIES OF SPARTA

History Books for Age 7-9
Children's History Books

BABY PROFESSOR

EDUCATION KIDS

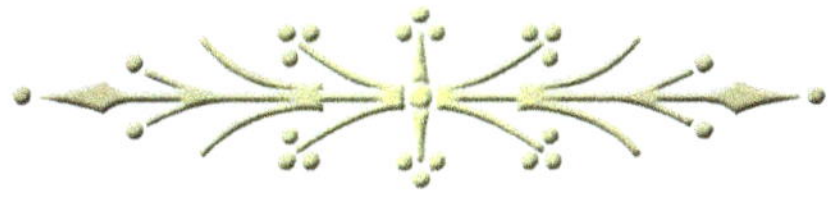

In Ancient Greek, the city-states would often fight one another. Occasionally, assemblies of city-states would join to fight with other assemblies of city-states in larger wars. On occasion the Greek city-states would unite to battle a shared enemy like the Persians in the Persian Wars.

Sparta was known to be the most commanding city-states in Ancient Greece. This was due to its strong army and the battles that occurred with the city-state Athens throughout the Peloponnesian War. It was located in a valley along the Eurotas River in the southeast of Greece.

SPARTA

Pyrrhus of Epirus

Sparta gained its power approximately 650 BC. They commanded the Greek city-states war from 492 BC to 449 BC with the Persians. During these wars, they battled in the infamous Battle of Thermopylae when 300 Spartans fended thousands of the Persians which then allowed the escape of the Greek Army.

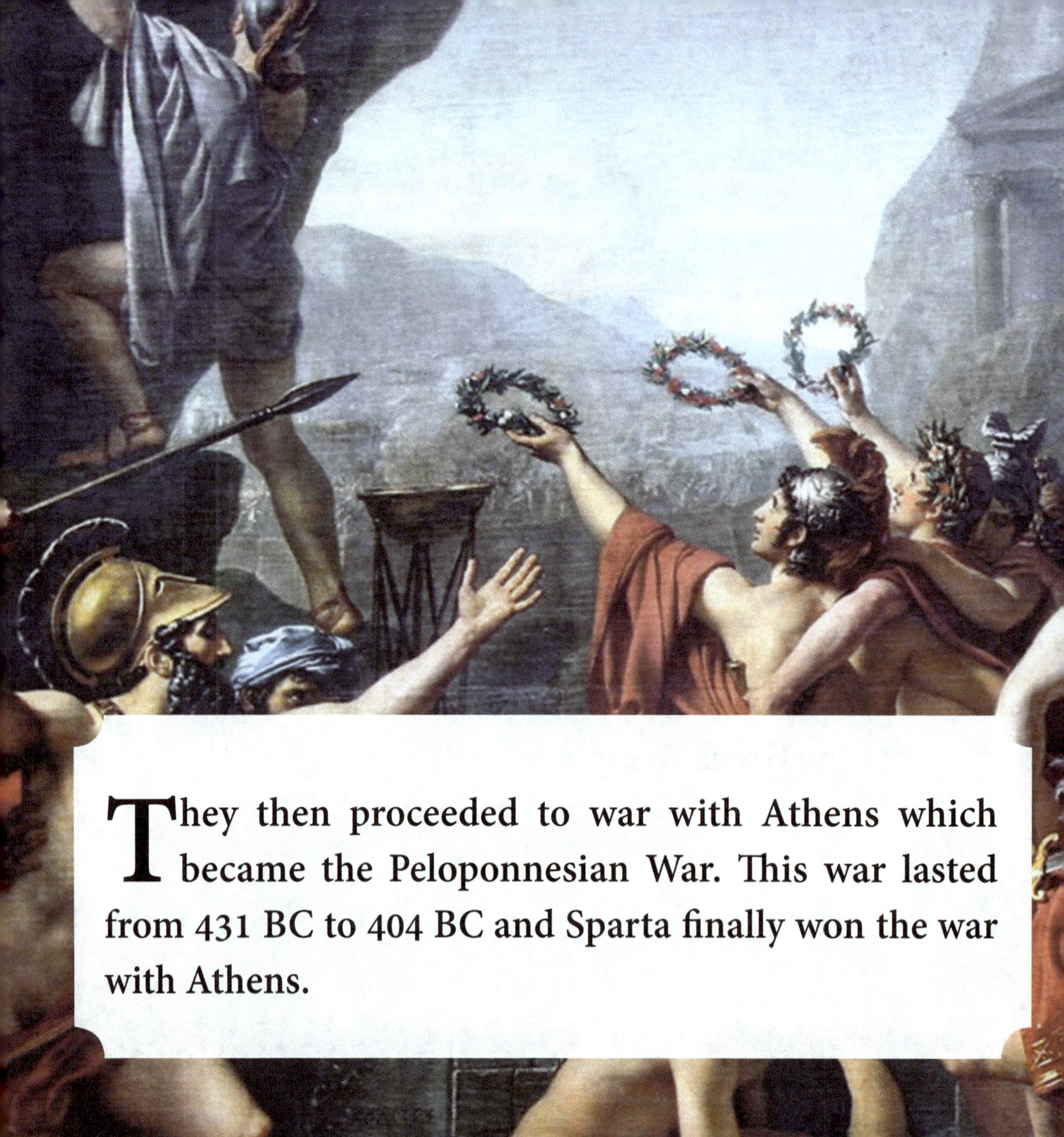

They then proceeded to war with Athens which became the Peloponnesian War. This war lasted from 431 BC to 404 BC and Sparta finally won the war with Athens.

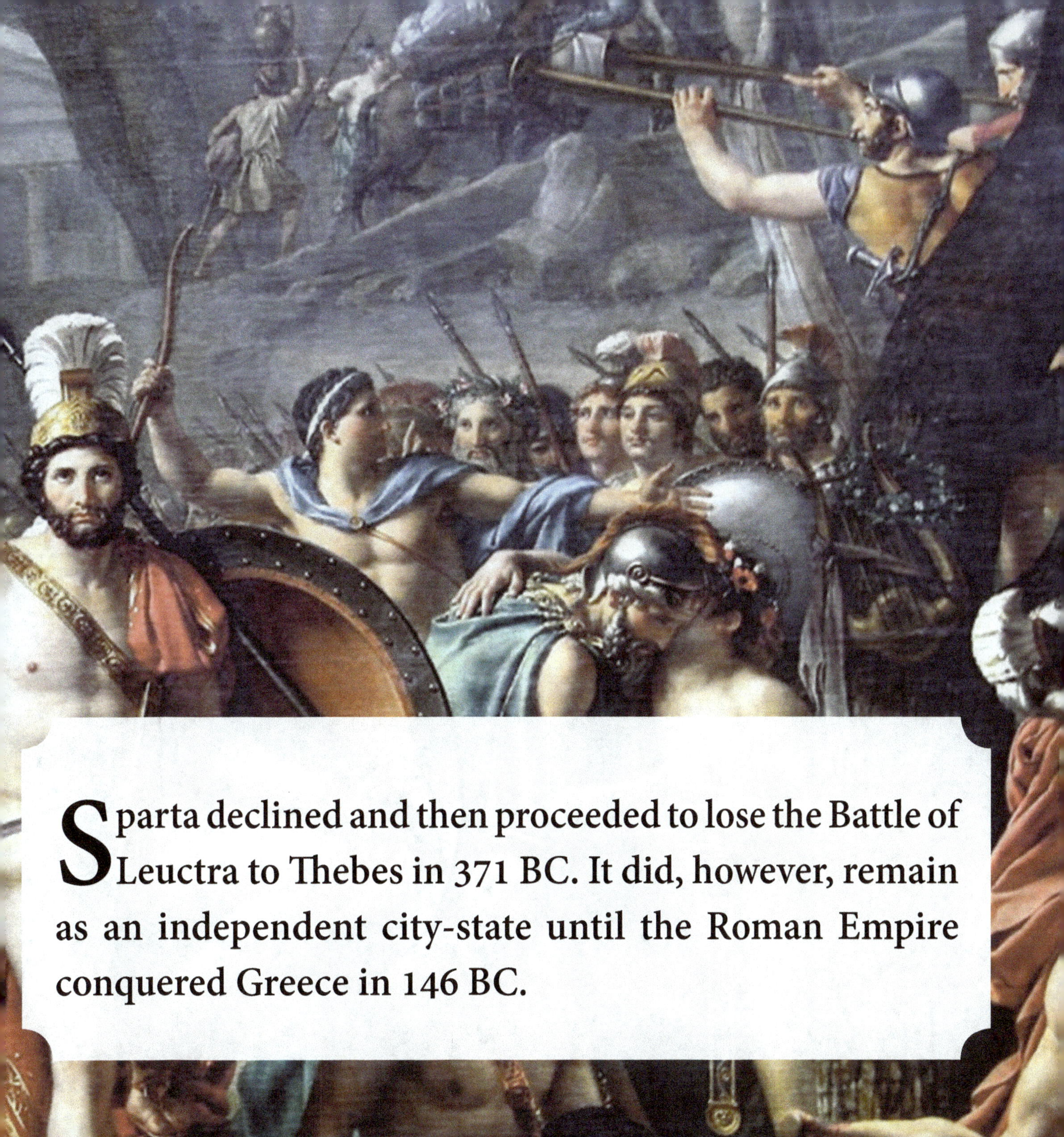

Sparta declined and then proceeded to lose the Battle of Leuctra to Thebes in 371 BC. It did, however, remain as an independent city-state until the Roman Empire conquered Greece in 146 BC.

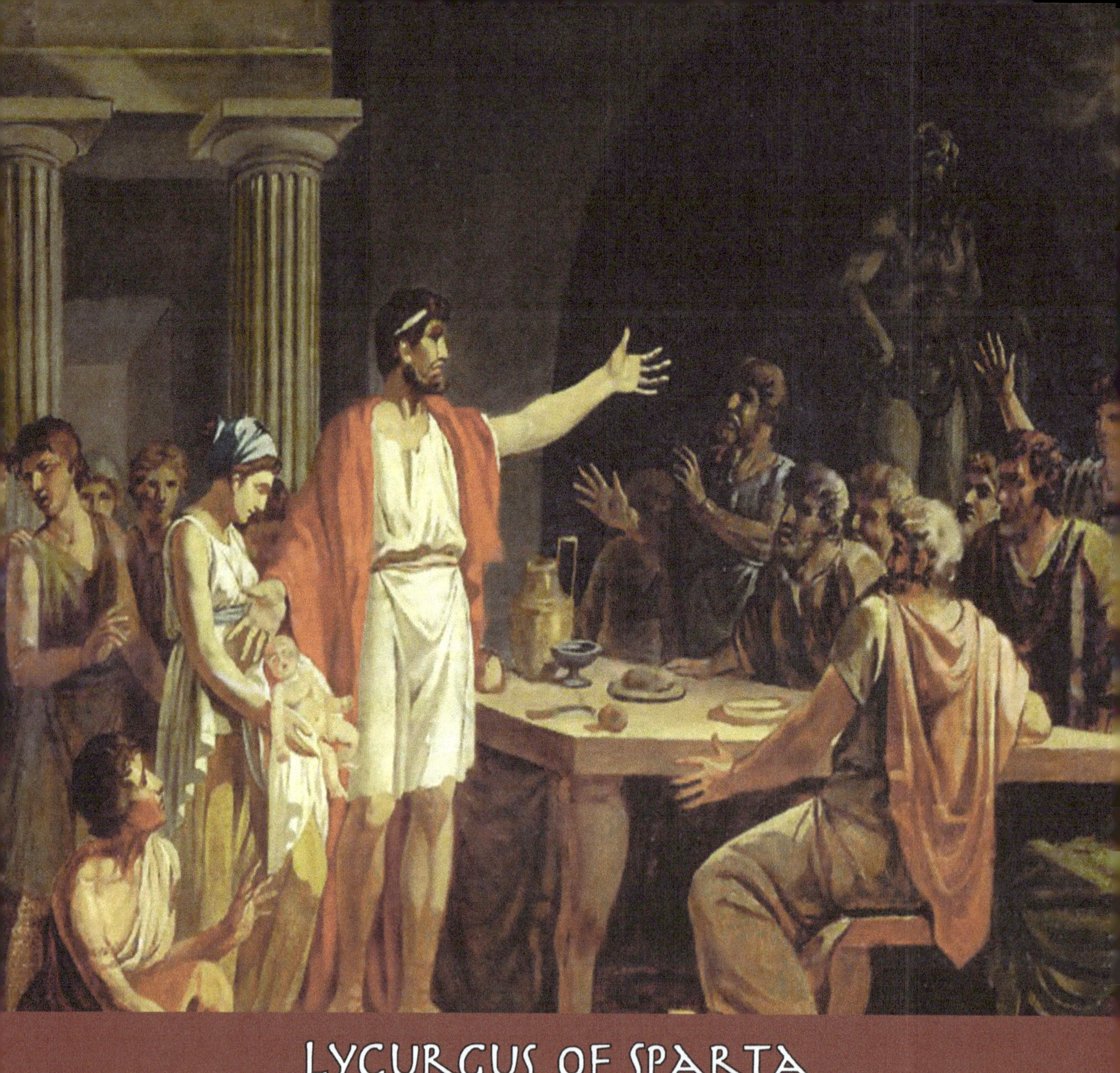

LYCURGUS OF SPARTA

Who Were They?

· · · · · · · · · · · · · · ·

The men that lived in a Greek city-state had to battle in their army. Most of the time they would not soldiers full time. They were men that owned a business or land and were fighting to protect the property they owned.

WEAPONS AND ARMOR

They were each required to purchase their weapons and armor. Typically, a wealthier soldier would have better weapons and armor. A set would include greaves to protect their shins, a helmet, a shield, and a bronze breastplate. Most of them would carry a doru, which was a long spear and a xiphos, which was a short sword.

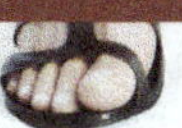

A SPARTAN WARRIOR

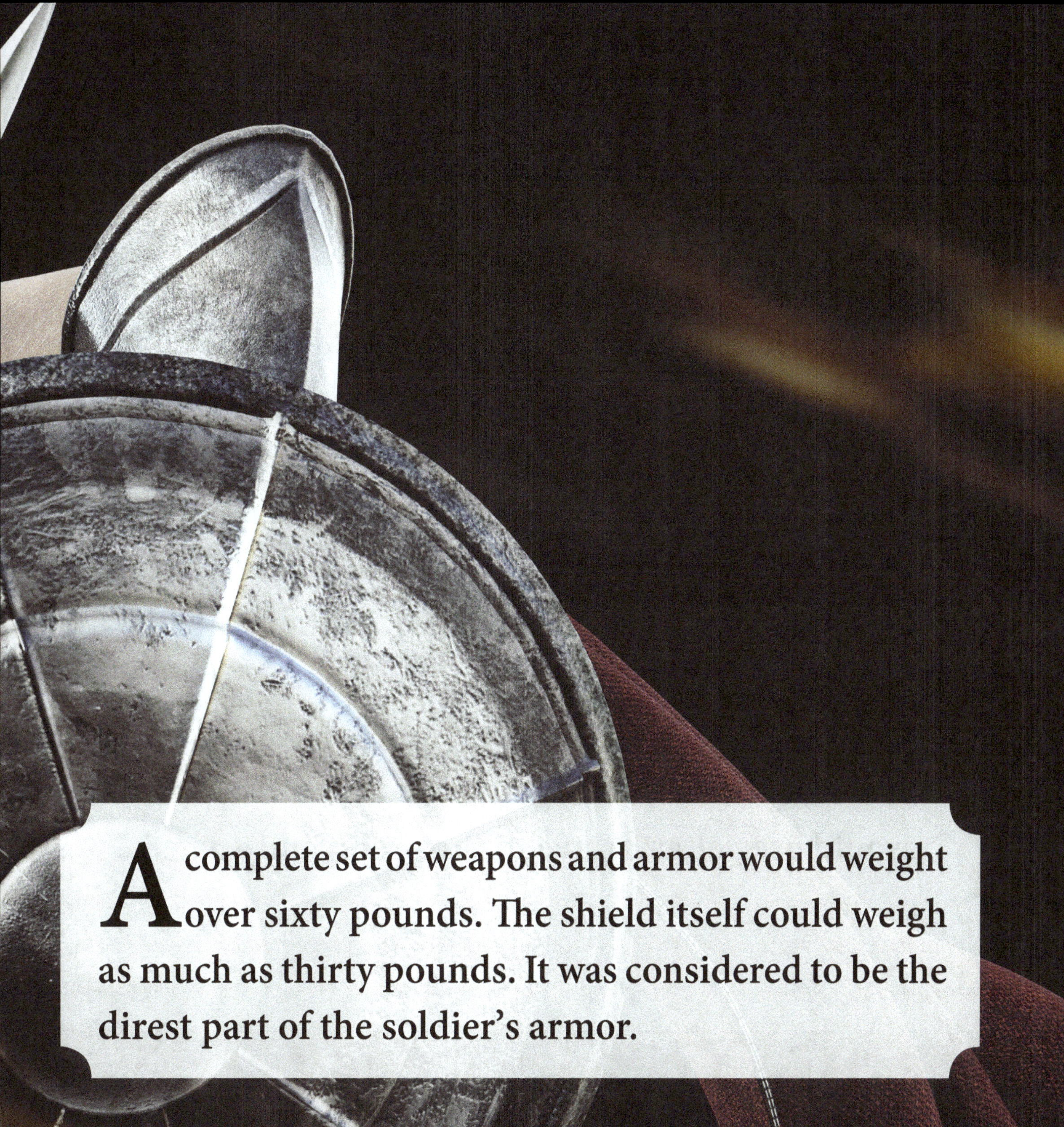

A complete set of weapons and armor would weight over sixty pounds. The shield itself could weigh as much as thirty pounds. It was considered to be the direst part of the soldier's armor.

If a soldier lost their shield during battle, it was a major disgrace. Legend states that their mothers would tell them to return "with their shield or on it". "On it" indicated that they were dead as the soldiers that had died would be brought home on top of their shields. Greek soldiers would sometimes decorate their shields. A common symbol they would put on the shields of the Athens soldiers consisted of a small owl and it represented the goddess Athena. They also would use peltasts (javelin throwers) and archers.

A SPARTAN WARRIOR WEARING
A BATTLE SHIELD AND WEAPON

What is a Hoplite?

The predominant soldier was a foot soldier that went by the name of "hoplite." They would carry long spears and large shields. They word "hoplite" stems from "hoplon", which is how they referred to their shield.

PHALANX

The "phalanx" was a formation used during battle. In this formation, they would be standing side to side with their shields overlapping which created a wall for protection. They would then march forward and use the spears when attacking their opponent.

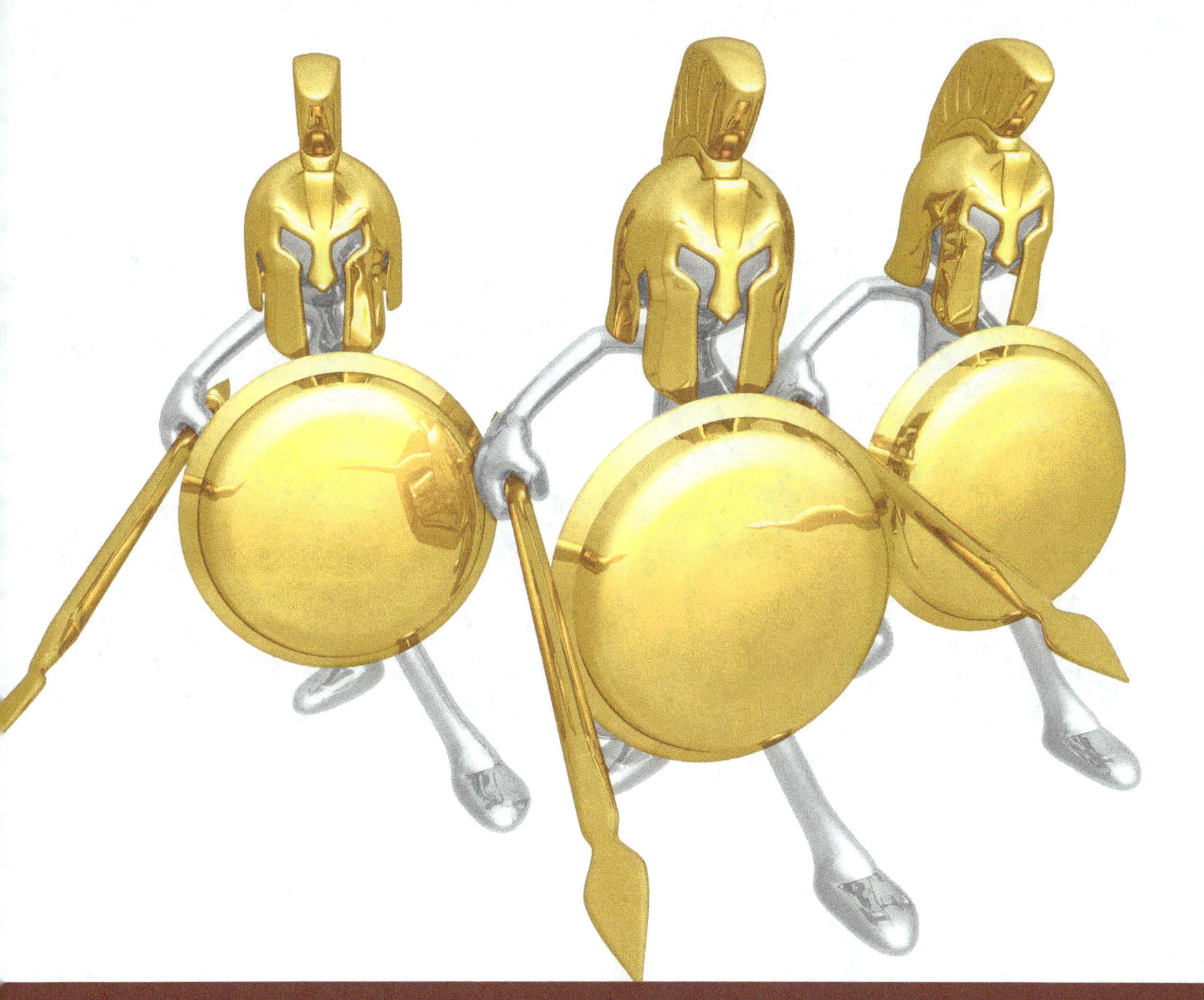

PHALANX

THE MACEDONIAN PHALANX

There would generally be many rows of the soldiers. The soldiers that were in the back would brace the ones in the front and would make them move forward. As two phalanxes would come together during battle, their goal would be to break the enemy's phalanx.

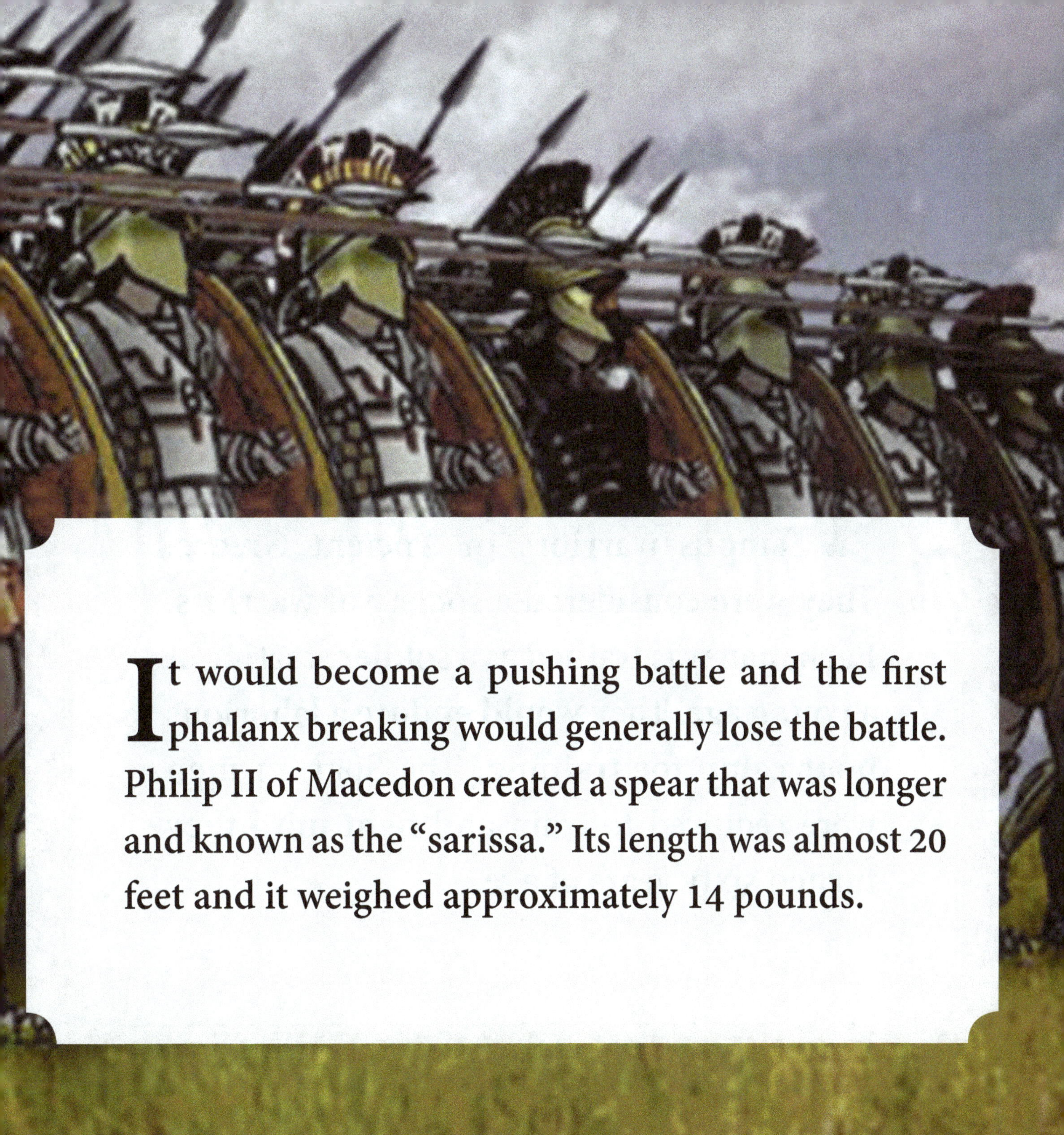

It would become a pushing battle and the first phalanx breaking would generally lose the battle. Philip II of Macedon created a spear that was longer and known as the "sarissa." Its length was almost 20 feet and it weighed approximately 14 pounds.

Sparta's Army

. . . .

The Spartans were the fiercest and most famous warriors in Ancient Greece. They were considered a society of warriors. Each man was trained as a soldier starting at a young age. They would endure a laborious boot camp for training. The Spartan men were required to train and fight until they turned sixty years of age.

SPARTA'S ARMY

Fighting at Sea

Since they lived along the Aegean Sea, they became experts when ship building. The trireme was one the main ships that was used for battle. On each side, there were three banks of oars and this allowed 170 rowers to power it. This power made it very quick during battle.

Greek bireme.   About

The bronze prow was considered to be the foremost weapon on a ship. It was located in the front of the ship and was used similar to a battering ram. They would ram it into an enemy's ship, which would make it sink.

THE PELOPONNESIAN WAR

The Peloponnesian War was fought between the Greek city-states of Sparta and Athens and began in 431 BC and ended in 404 BC. Athens lost the war, end the golden age of Ancient Greece. The word Peloponnesian arises out of the name of a peninsula in southern Greece named the Peloponnese.

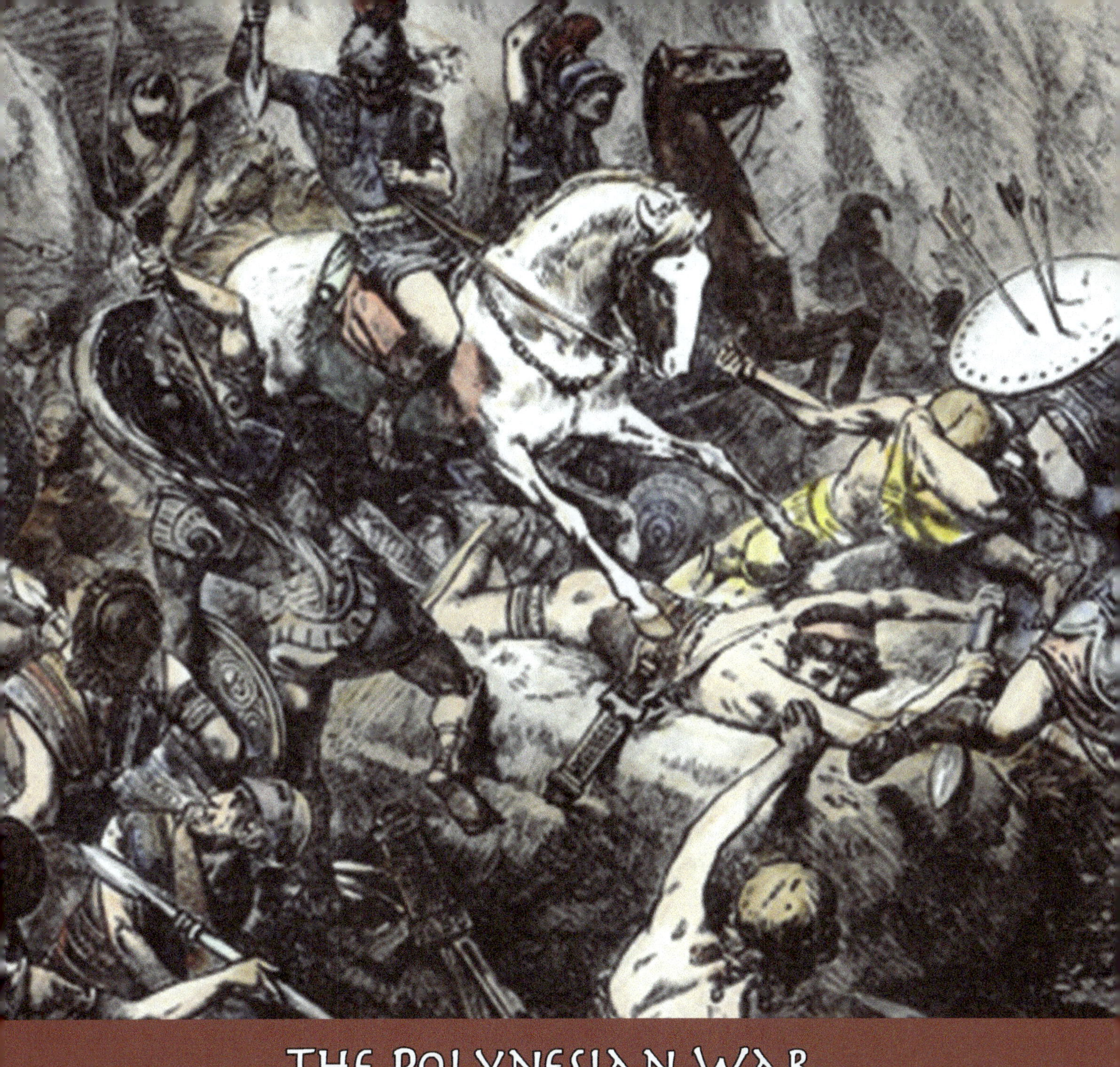

THE POLYNESIAN WAR

Many of the distinguished Greek city-states were located on this peninsula, including Messene, Sparta, Corinth, and Argos. The first key war that occurred between Athens and Sparta is sometimes referred to as the Archidamian War after Sparta's King Archidamus II.

The Greek soldiers were named hoplites. They would typically fight with a spear, shields, and a short sword.

Prior to the War

Sparta and Athens agreed to a Thirty Year Peace after the Persian War. They did not want to fight as they were recovering from the Persian War. Athens proceeded to become wealthy and powerful and its empire grew under Pericles leadership.

BAZAR OF ATHENS

Thebes defeated Sparta in 371 BC in a war known as the Battle of Leuctra. Sparta and its allies started to become more and more distrustful and jealous of Athens.

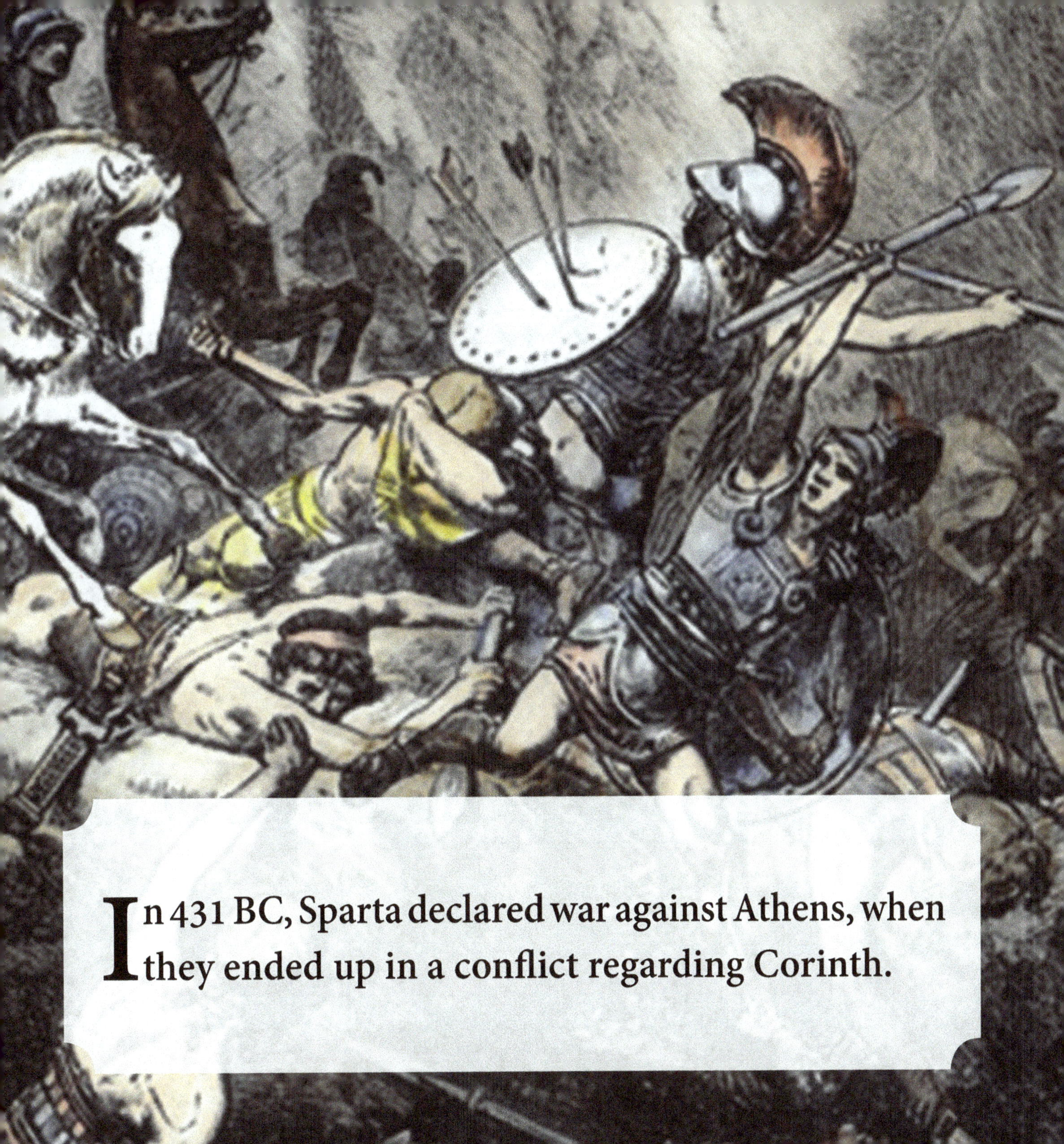

In 431 BC, Sparta declared war against Athens, when they ended up in a conflict regarding Corinth.

BATTLE OF SALAMIS (306 BC)

THE FIRST WAR

· · · · · · · · · · · · ·

The first Peloponnesian War lasted ten years. It was at this time that the Spartans controlled the land and the Athenians controlled the sea. Athens then constructed long walls that went from the city to the seaport Piraeus. This then made it possible for them to stay in the city and still be able to have access to supplies and trade among their ships.

While they never penetrated the walls of Athens during this war, many people inside the city died because of the plague. Included in these deaths was Pericles, the leader and general of Athens.

Athens' long walls were approximately 4 ½ miles long. The total length of the walls that surrounded the city and its ports was about 22 miles.

ATHENS' LONG WALLS

SOLON THE WISE LAW GIVER

PEACE OF NICIAS

After the war, in 421 BC Athens and Sparta came to a truce. It was named the Peace of Nicias, after the Athenian army general.

Athens Attacks Sicily

In 415 BC, Athens wanted to assist one of their partners on the island of Sicily. They proceeded to send a large force to attack Syracuse. Athens then lost this battle terribly and Sparta then decided to retaliate which became the Second Peloponnesian War.

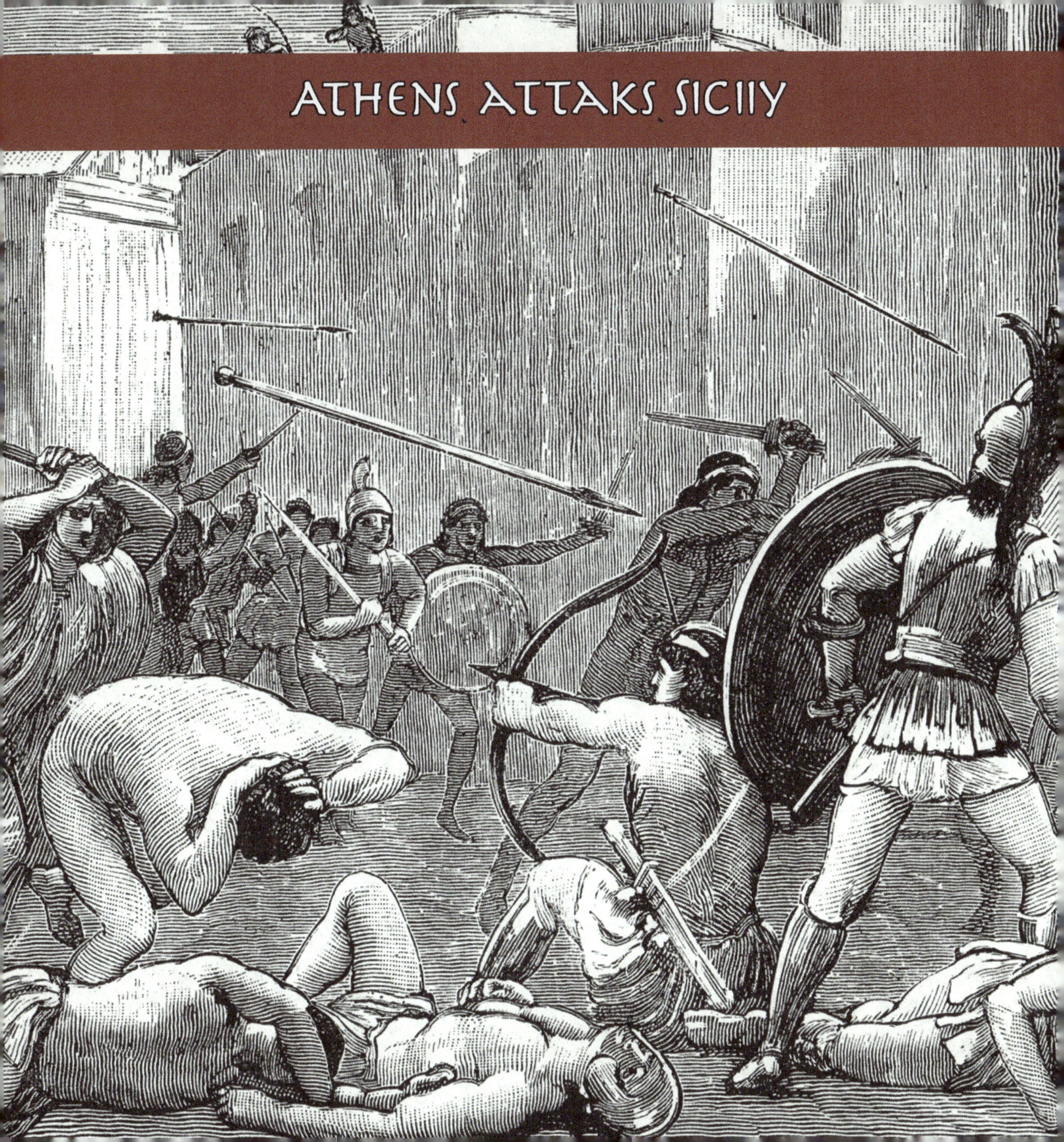

ATHENS ATTAKS SICIIY

THE SECOND WAR

The Second War

The Spartans then proceeded to assemble allies to conquer Athens. They even went as far as to enlist help from the Persians who lent money to then so that they could build a fleet of ships for war. However, Athens recovered and won the battles which occurred between 410 and 406 BC.

Athens is Defeated

General Lysander, of the Spartan army went on to defeat Athens in 405 BC. With the Athenian fleet defeated, people of Athens began starving. They had no army to fight the Spartans on land. Athens then surrendered to Sparta in 404 BC. Thebes and Corinth wanted Athens destroyed and enslaved. Sparta did not agree with this. They made them take its walls down, refusing to destroy its city or enslave the people.

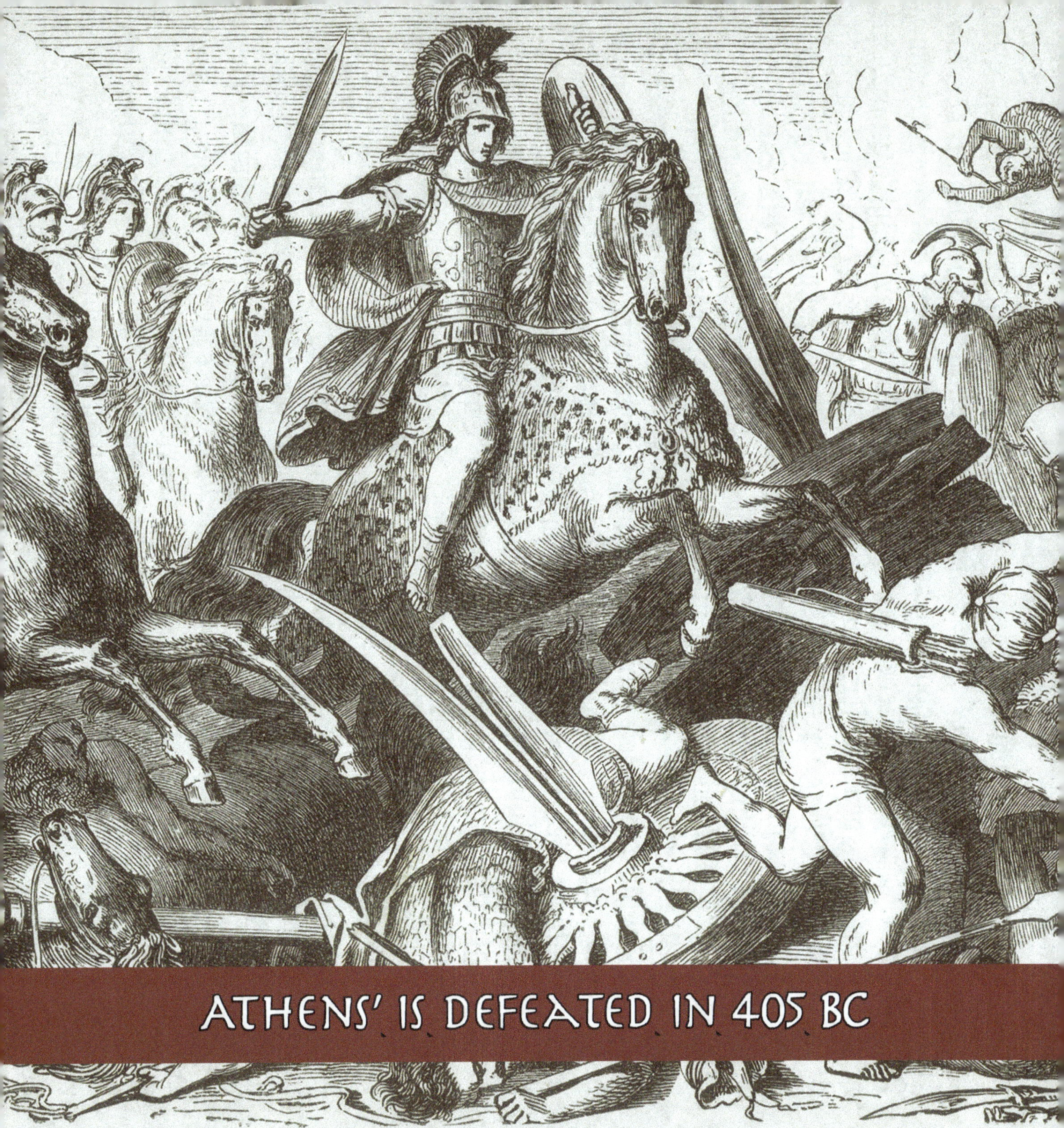

ATHENS' IS DEFEATED IN 405 BC

Once Sparta conquered Athens, they put an end to democracy and started a new government governed by the "Thirty Tyrants". However, this lasted

for only one year since the local Athenians defeated
these tyrants and democracy was restored.

What Was It Like to Grow Up as a Boy in Sparta?

The boys would be trained as soldiers starting in their youth. Until they were seven, they would be raised by their mother but then would have to enter the Agoge, which was a military school. Here the boys would be trained to fight in addition to learning to read and write. It was a tough school.

The boys would live in barracks and often would be beaten to increase their toughness. In order to know what life would be like at war, they were given very little to eat. They were encouraged to fight each other. Once they became 20 they would have to enter the Spartan Army.

What Was It Like to Grow Up as a Girl in Sparta?

The girls would start school when they turned seven. While their school was not as difficult, they trained in exercise and athletics. It was important for them to stay in shape so their sons would be strong and able to fight. The women had more freedoms than most of the other Greek city-states during this time period. They would usually marry at 18.

For more information about Sparta and Ancient Greek, research the internet, go to your local library, and ask questions of your teachers, family, and friends.

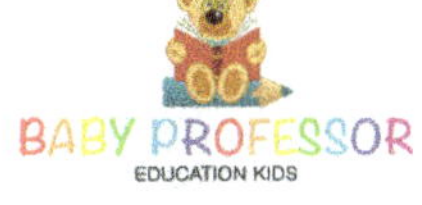